Life Skills Primer
Essays on Leadership

Edited By

GEORGE W. RIDEOUT, D.B.A.

Dedication

For tomorrow's leaders...

Contents

Foreword

Young people in the twenty-first century face a complex world creating challenges unthinkable even twenty years ago. Challenges such as a global economy, social and cultural change, and the incessant pace of technological growth create a muddy environment for anyone living on our planet, including experienced adults! Whatever our cultural, ethnic, or social background, we face similar challenges and must learn to cope, not only to gain a competitive advantage, but also to survive.

I have yet to meet a parent, regardless of race or ethnic origin, who does not want something better for his or her children. Most parents, even with their grand dreams, just want their kids to grow up healthy and live a happy life. Having each child become a good citizen who makes a positive contribution to society even in the simplest form is a part of this desire. Is this too much to ask? I think not. The problem is that achieving this, given the brood of challenges evident in twenty-first century society, demands new skills, including a new way of thinking. These survival skills resonate the complexity of society, and I am sure will continue to evolve as we dig deeper into the twenty-first century.

Remember the old proverb *give a man a fish feed him for a day, but teach a man to fish and feed him for a lifetime*? This proverb distills the true meaning of what represents a life skill. Life skills are not about temporary fixes or doing what is best for today. Life skills are about long-term positive change, which can provide a foundation for a healthy productive life. That is the impetus for this book; to identify skills needed for long-term success given the challenges evident in early twenty-first century society.

This book by no means covers the entire range of skills needed for today or the future but does offer a foundation. From discussions on emotional intelligence and entrepreneurship to appreciation of lifestyle differences, Life Skills Primer provides a starting point, perhaps a guiding light for others in the field of academia that wishes to explore modern life skill challenges. More important, this book creates much needed dialogue about what I think is one of the greatest challenges facing society, educating our young people to become productive and responsible leaders. Whether you are an educator or parent, this book is of interest to you. Although written from a scholarly perspective, the book is an easy interesting read for anyone.

I challenge you to consider the young people in your life. Consider the influence you have on them. Ponder the challenges you see in society, and develop your own list of life skills. I am sure your list will become a valuable extension of what is in this book. Take your list and groom it. More important use it as a tool to help the young people in your life.

---*George W. Rideout*

Life Skills Primer
Essays on Leadership

1 Emotional Intelligence for Leaders

Matthew Alcindor

Ensuring the perpetuity and viability of organizations is a challenge to organizational leaders who, according to the Center for Creative Leadership (CCL) surveys, understand leadership in the future will call for new skill sets (Smith, 2010). Some employees appear to have innate management and leadership abilities; developing that ability is a human resource investment valuable to the organization in the short and long-term (Messmer, 1999). Business leaders understand the ongoing development of employees is a necessity, yet the majority of workers in organizations don't engage in skill development activities (Kaye, 2010). Employee development is a priority requiring organizational leaders to facilitate "skills growth" by engaging employees in activities that increase learning (Hameed & Waheed, 2011). Learning should enhance leadership skills, efficiency, and productivity. Emotional intelligence (EI) is a competency business, and educational leaders need to develop in employees.

Emotional Intelligence (EI)

Salovey and Mayer (1990) introduced the concept of EI. Prior to the early 1990s, EI did not receive widespread attention because researchers focused on the role cognitive intelligence played in the workplace (Carmeli, 2003). Salovey and Mayer defined EI as the accurate perception, regulation, and management of emotions. Goleman (1995) highlighted the importance of researching employee emotions and found EI to be essential for effective leadership, teamwork, and management of relationships. Chopra and Kanji (2010) pointed to research showing intellect to be composed of multiple intelligences in different parts of the brain. Chopra and Kanji described EI as social intelligence, a concept rooted in Gardner's (1983) theory of multiple intelligences. Brain research reveals emotions and logic are interconnected because decision-making involves engaging the emotional part of the brain (Sparrow & Knight, 2006). Chopra and Kanji mentioned research showing EI as a better indicator of excellence than general intelligence, being a key to self-management, developing human potential, relationship management, leadership, job performance, organizational development, and educational development. EI now

2

has become seen as a competency that is vital to the successful leadership and performance of individuals and groups in various organizational settings.

Business Organizations

Leadership skill and competency requirements in businesses have changed in the last two decades. The managerial responsibilities of good performance and establishing healthy relationships were once considered governed by cognitive intelligences; Bostjancic (2010) now considers them centered in EI. Many researchers suggest EI is critical because they see emotional and behavioral flexibility as the hallmark of a skilled manager (Goleman, 1995). According to Bostjancic, EI influences jobs satisfaction and is vital for jobs centered in human interaction. Bostjancic suggested leaders exhibiting high levels of EI are more successful in the workplace, being viewed as good listeners sensitive to others' views. Like the natural systems thinkers, researchers in global business operations see the critical importance of understanding the human aspects of the organization. Global business leaders, who once saw success linked to hard data, rational decision-making, and technology, see the need for a healthy balance of cognitive intelligence and EI to drive successful business outcomes (Colfax, Rivera, & Perez, 2010).

Demir (2011) suggested EI has a positive relationship to decreasing deviant behavior in the workplace and decreasing turnover. Demir highlighted EI as contributing to a high quality of work life while diminishing deviances such as showing favoritism, workplace gossiping, sexual harassment, stealing, taking long breaks, lying on time sheets, and sabotage. Singh (2010) asserted EI is a popular concept in managerial science, requiring its understanding in enhancing human capital. According to Singh, rapid change and increased demand on organizational leadership's emotional resources make EI an essential component for effective management.

Educational Settings

Researchers view EI as a tool with relevance to educational organizations (Ignat, 2010). Ignat stated teachers facing social stressors are responsible for the development of children; they need EI to manage, reduce, control, and cope with these stressors. Ghanizadeh and Moafian (2010) found evidence supporting positive correlations between EI and teacher success. According to

4

Ghanizadeh and Moafian, EI enhances learning by helping teachers establish healthy rapport, create a warm atmosphere, and manage personal relationships. Emotional well-being has taken on importance in classroom settings. According to McLaughlin (2008), some researchers feel the ability to manage and calm the individual self is learned at critical stages in childhood and early adolescence; it is linked to positive, sensitive, caring, and supportive relationships between teachers and students.

Research suggests EI influences the quality of education received by children in classroom settings (Birol, Atamturk, Silman, & Sensoy, 2009). Learning is a social process affected by emotional competency in educational social settings; EI is believed to influence teachers' performance (Mustafa & Amjad, 2011). Mustafa and Amjad suggested teachers with high levels of EI exhibit proper emotions and diligently work to enhance student learning. Bardach (2008) highlighted middle school success linking to high levels of EI among school principals, and school systems benefiting from training school principals in EI.

Foster Care Agencies

Child welfare/foster care supervisors and case managers are vulnerable to high stress, burnout, and job dissatisfaction because of their demanding responsibilities (Strolin, McCarthy, & Caringi, 2007). Maintaining proper relationships to offset the psychological and emotional stressors faced in the workplace is critical to leadership success. Graen and Uhl-Bien (1995) found leader member exchange theory (LMX) to be a relationship-based approach to leadership characterized by supervisory support and two-way communication. LMX is based upon exchanges in the relationship between leaders and subordinates; it postulates support, fairness, and the recognition of individual uniqueness, resulting in reciprocal commitment and loyalty to the organization (Camplin, 2009). EI is viewed as a competency rooted in social intelligence and essential to leaders maintaining and managing healthy relationships leading to efficient performance (Huang, Chan, Lam, & Nan, 2010). High quality LMX in the workplace can be a reality if leadership has, and knows how to apply, EI.

Foster care agencies rely on and expect case managers and supervisors exhibiting organizational citizenship behavior (OCB).

Foster care agencies rely on case managers working long hours. Helping peers, volunteering for extra work, working without complaint, maintaining punctuality, promoting the organization, and observing regulations are examples of OCB (Turnipseed & Wilson, 2009). Peelle (2007) described OCB as discretionary behavior performed outside of normal job functions benefiting the organization, yet going without formal recognition. People who perceive high levels of organizational fairness are more likely to engage in OCB, feeling indebted to the organization, whereas perceptions of interpersonal injustice will lead to unfavorable reactions and responses toward the immediate supervisor (Cho & Kessler, 2008).

EI influences the amounts of OCB exhibited by participants (Yaghoubi, Mashinchi, & Hadi, 2011). Understanding, empathy, and support result in reciprocating loyalty and commitment to the organization (Chen & Chiu, 2008). Casework supervisors handling these staff need EI competency to assist staff in handling the job stress and complexities; staff EI competency also helps maintain the psychological hardiness in routine engagement of OCB vital to the overall maintenance of the system.

Conclusions

Organizational leaders should incorporate EI in their training and development programs for managers. EI is now understood to play a pivotal role in employees' reaching their full development potential (Chester, 2004). Chester pointed out how organizational leaders can benefit from (a) obtaining an EI assessment identifying their individual emotional intelligence quotient (EQ), and (b) investing in EI coaching programs strengthening leadership ability to balance emotional and organizational demands in the workplace. Investment in the assessment and development of EI for organizational leaders is needed to sustain competitive advantage, maintain harmonious and healthy work environments, and bring out the full range of job potential in employees. Educational and social work settings, characterized by high levels of social activity and interaction, need leaders who can balance the exposure to stress and trauma; thus, EI is a necessary component of training and development programs. To strengthen existing research on the influence, impact, and implication of EI in business, foster care, and educational settings, future research could be geared toward evaluating organizational and managerial performance after participation in EI assessment,

training, and development programs.

References

Bardach, R. H. (2008). *Leading schools with emotional intelligence: A study of the degree of association between middle school principal emotional intelligence and school success.* Capella University. Available from ProQuest Dissertation and Theses database. (3289486)

Birol, C., Atamturk, H., Silman, F., & Sensoy, S. (2009). Analysis of emotional intelligence level of teachers. *Procedia, Social and Behavioral Science, 1,* 2606-2614. doi: 10.1016/j.sbspro.2009.01.460

Bostjancic, E. (2010). Personality, job satisfaction, and performance of Slovenia managers–How big is the role of emotional intelligence in this? *Studia Psychologica, 52*(3), 207-218.

Camplin, J. C. (2009). Volunteers leading volunteers. *Professional Safety, 54*(5), 36-42.

Carmeli, A. (2003). The relationship between emotional intelligence and work attitudes, behavior and outcomes: An examination among senior managers. *Journal of Managerial Psychology, 18*(7/8), 788-813.

Chen, C. C., & Chiu, S. F. (2008). An integrative model linking supervisory support and organizational citizenship behaviors. *Journal of Business and Psychology, 23*(1-2), 237-244. doi: 10.1007/s10869-008-9084-y

Chester, P. (2004). Fitting emotional intelligence into leadership coaching. *Human Resources Magazine, 9*(5), 18-19.

Cho, J., & Kessler, S. R. (2008). Employee's distributive justice perceptions and organizational citizenship behaviors: A social exchange perspective. *Review of Business Research, 8*(6), 131-137.

Chopra, P. K., & Kanji, G. K. (2010). Emotional intelligence: A catalyst for inspirational leadership and management excellence. *Total Quality Management & Business Excellence, 21*(10), 971-1004. doi: 10.1080/14783363.2010.487704

Colfax, R. S., Rivera, J. J., & Perez, K. T. (2010). Applying emotional intelligence (EQ-I) in the workplace: Vital to global success. *Journal Of International Business Research, 9,* 89-98.

Demir, M. (2011). The analysis of the relationship among emotional intelligence, organizational deviance, quality of work life, and turnover intentions in hospitality business. *European Journal Of Tourism Research, 4*(2), 214-216.

Gardner, H. (1983). *Frames of mind: The theory of multiple intelligences.* New York, NY: Basic Books.

Ghanizadeh, A., & Moafian, F. (2010). The role of EFL teachers' emotional intelligence in their success. *ELT Journal, 64*(4), 424-435.

Goleman, D. (1995). *Emotional intelligence: Why it can matter more than IQ.* New York, NY: Bantam Books.

Graen, G. B., & Uhl-Bien. M. (1995). Relationship based approach to leadership: Development of leader member exchange (LMX) theory of leadership over 25 years: Applying a multi-level multi-domain perspective. *The Leadership Quarterly, 6*(2), 219-247.

Hameed, A., & Waheed, A. (2011). Employee development and its affect on employee performance: A conceptual framework. *International Journal Of Business & Social Science, 2*(13), 224-229.

Huang, X., Chan, S. H., Lam, W., & Nan, X. (2010). The joint effect of leader-member exchange and emotional intelligence on burnout and work performance in call centers in China. *The International Journal Of Human Resource Management, 21*(7), 1124-1144.

Ignat, A. (2010). Teachers' satisfaction with life, emotional intelligence, and stress reactions. *Petroleum-Gas University Of Ploiesti Bulletin, Educational Sciences Series, 62*(2), 32-41.

Kaye, B. (2010). IDP 2.0: The future of the development dialogue. *T+D, 64*(12), 52.

McLaughlin, C. (2008). Emotional well-being and its relationship to schools and classrooms: A critical reflection. *British Journal of Guidance & Counseling, 36*(4), 353-366.

Messmer, M. (1999). Building leadership skills. *Strategic Finance, 81*(1), 10-12.

Mustafa, L., & Amjad, S. (2011). Emotional intelligence determining work attitudes and outcomes of university teachers: Evidence from Pakistan. *Interdisciplinary Journal of Contemporary Research In Business, 2*(10), 240-259.

Peelle, III, H. E. (2007). Reciprocating perceived organizational support through citizenship behaviors. *Journal of Management Issues, 19*(4), 554-578.

Salovey, P., & Mayer, J. (1990). Emotional intelligence. *Imagination, cognition, and personality, 9*(3), 185-211.

Singh, K. (2010). Developing human capital by linking emotional intelligence with personal competencies in Indian business organizations. *International Journal of Business Science and Applied Management, 5*(2), 29-42.

Smith, D. (2010). A leadership skills gap? *T+D, 64*(2), 16-17.

Sparrow, T., & Knight, A. (2006). *Applied emotional intelligence.* Chichester, West Sussex, UK: John Wiley & Sons.

Strolin, J. S., McCarthy, M., & Caringi, J. (2007). Causes and effects of child welfare workforce turnover: Current state of knowledge and future directions. *Journal of Public Child Welfare, 1*(2), 29-52.

Turnipseed, D. L., & Wilson, G. L. (2009). From discretionary to required: The migration of organizational citizenship behavior. *Journal of Leadership & Organizational Studies, 15*(3), 201-217.

Yaghoubi, E., Mashinchi, S., & Hadi, A. (2011). An analysis of correlation between organizational citizenship behavior (OCB) and emotional intelligence (EI). *Modern Applied Science, 5*(2), 119-123.

2 Steps Toward Implementing Gay Themes: Personal Reflection and Recommendations for Action

Gabriel Flores

In the United States in 2000, 16% of all hate crimes were directed toward gay and lesbian people (Ventura, Lambert, Bryant, & Pasupuleti, 2004). Types of hate crimes included murder, manslaughter, rape, aggravated assault, simple assault, intimidation, arson, and damage or vandalism of property (Willis, 2004). In addition, gay or lesbian individuals committed nearly one third of all suicides in the United States (Allan, 1999; Daniel, 2007; Satterly & Dyson, 2005; Van Wormer & McKinney, 2003). A multicultural curriculum teaching tolerance and diversity towards homosexuals may reduce hate crimes, suicides, and fear, and in turn, create meaningful change within society (Hansman, 1998; Milton, 2003).

Teaching tolerance and acceptance about sexual orientation can never start too early (Lai, 2006; Roffman, 2001; Solomon, 2004;

Woody, 2002); however, huge misconceptions exist. One

misconception is that gay themes and gay-themed children's

literature is age-inappropriate in the elementary classroom and that

discussions involve sexual behavior. The aforementioned point

demonstrates a need for schools, districts, and educational leaders

to provide appropriate training to teachers who express the

misconception. The goal of teaching gay issues is not to convert or

influence students, but to educate and create tolerance and

environments free of harassment, homophobia, and discrimination

(Wolfe, 2006). Implementing gay themes in the classroom through

professional development and pedagogical training may bring

about a safer learning environment for all children, including gay

youth, by reducing intolerance and bullying and increasing

acceptance and student achievement. Unfortunately, public schools

have been slow to implement gay themes as a part of a balanced

multicultural education curriculum (Giugni & Semann, 2004; Moita-

Lopes, 2006; Swartz, 2003).

In the following paragraphs, some steps and ideas for

educators and school leaders are provided that may serve to help

with the implementation process. I will also reflect on my

14

experiences as an educator who has implemented gay themes in the elementary classroom since 2002. Before describing the steps, however, some historical background is essential.

During the 1980s and 1990s, multicultural education focused on inclusion of Asian, African-American, and/or Latino cultural themes in the multicultural classroom. In 1992, gay culture was included as part of the multicultural education agenda for classrooms by the National Association of Multicultural Education (NAME). During the new millennium, teachers were encouraged by multicultural education scholars to implement a more diverse multicultural education curriculum that incorporates gay-themed children's literature (i.e. two-daddy or two-mommy families, transgender, and gender nonconformance characters) in the elementary classroom (NAME, 2005a, 2005b). Unfortunately, many teachers are dissuaded from implementing gay themes, usually by fears of retaliation, by parents and administrators, or the teachers' negative attitudes.

Research has suggested, however, that attending in-service and professional development training has helped improve negative attitudes and dispel misconceptions about the lesbian, gay, bisexual, and transsexual community (Bowen & Bourgeois, 2001; Maher, 2007). It is important teachers be made aware the right-wing movement, religious organizations, and some politicians may object to gay theme implementation, but micro-revolutionary changes can occur by teachers and administrators attending training sessions, having discussions, and accepting and advocating gays and lesbians' civil rights (Barber & Krane, 2007; Birden, 2002; Lucas, 2004). Incorporating sexual orientation and gay culture into diversity workshops may help sensitize and educate staff, faculty members, students, and administrators (Barber & Krane, 2007; Cosier & Sanders, 2007; Moita-Lopes, 2006; Swartz, 2003). Providing such support may create a more successful program for implementing gay-themed literature in the classroom.

Research has found schools, districts, and pre-service university teacher programs are not including gay themes and issues into diversity education courses. In my own research (Flores, 2009), more than 80% of the teacher participants in the study demonstrated a lack of training in gay themes for the multicultural education classroom. As I previously suggested in that research, an initial step in implementing gay themes and gay-themed children's literature may be through professional development, both within school districts and in preservice teaching programs. It is important school districts provide training that exposes teachers to critical pedagogy theory because critical pedagogy is an important step in guiding teachers when implementing gay themes in the classroom. Because critical pedagogues question mainstream culture, counteract mainstream ideas, and help the subjugated within society (Chen, 2005), introducing the theory may be crucial for helping implement gay themes in the classroom environment. Once teachers understand that gays and lesbians comprise an underrepresented and subjugated minority (Hansman, 1998) who are at-risk (Skegg, 2005), a smoother transition towards implementing gay themes and gay-themed children's literature may be possible.

Within my elementary school setting, I conducted critical pedagogy professional development training in June 2007. The training, entitled "Critical Pedagogy Theory and Tolerance," involved teachers reading Chen (2005) and summarizing the elements about critical pedagogy theory. I believe that in order to have schools implement gay themes within a multicultural education program, teachers should learn about critical pedagogy and its relationship to gay themes and gay culture.

My elementary school is one that implements gay themes during June as part of celebrating Gay and Lesbian Awareness Month. My critical pedagogy training may have helped teachers make revolutionary changes within their own classrooms; I am one of 10 other teachers who implements gay themes to various age groups of children. In addition, my school library is one of the most diverse with many gay-themed children's literature included within its bookshelves. Teachers, administrators, and the librarian have ordered and welcomed the literature into the library's collection.

Teachers also require training about the contact theory hypothesis. Basset et al. (2005) found certain factors within the contact theory hypothesis reduced prejudice against gays, such as accepting a biological explanation for homosexuality, taking human sexuality classes, listening to gay guest speakers, exposing teachers to gay peers, and watching films that address prejudice against homosexuals. The basic premise behind the contact theory hypothesis is contact with lesbian, gay, bisexual, and transgender (LGBT) people lead to more tolerance and acceptance.

Because some people believe gay lifestyles are unnatural, it is important training focus on teaching tolerance and reducing homophobia. It is essential that school districts put into practice the contact theory hypothesis by implementing proficiency training in gay culture that includes the gay struggle and gay civil rights movement, gay familial awareness (two-mommy, two-daddy families), societal dangers for gays, and issues pertaining to gay youth at school. Training needs to be focused on the real life experiences of gays and lesbians and statistics about hate crimes and suicides among gay youth. In learning about the contact theory hypothesis, teachers may learn the facts about gays and that negative attitudes are based on fear and a lack of knowledge. Through education and training, teachers may slowly become more tolerant and accepting of gay people and implement gay themes and gay-themed children's literature in the classroom.

Crary (1992) suggested two methods to help deal with the differences and ensure children become comfortable with different types of people and cultures: First, introducing differences through children's books and literature and second, offering children experiences with real people. As an educator who has implemented gay themes in the classroom, I have introduced gay people and friends to my students, thus putting the contact theory hypothesis into practice.

I invited my openly gay friend to help me teach a division lesson. He helped the students with the lesson and was a funny guest: He made the math lesson fun. After he left, I casually mentioned that he was my gay friend Eddie. Children were shocked; I assume the children had a stereotyped image in their heads of a gay man. My friend Eddie is a masculine man with a deep voice and is handsome. A short discussion ensued about how he works, has a family, and loves his family/partner like anyone else. I believe it was a good learning experience for the students and dispelled many misconceptions; it was a chance for them to become more tolerant and accepting individuals. Some students expressed their misconceptions, and they were quite extraordinary.

Some teachers feel discomfort when teaching gay themes and do not teach sexual orientation education and gay themes due to their own intolerance (Athanases, 1996; Birden, 2002; Hermann-Wilmarth, 2007; Rienzo, Button, Jiunn-Jye, & Ying, 2006; Van Wormer & McKinney, 2003). However, such teachers would have to learn how to handle and or set aside their own feelings of discomfort and fear. The implication here is a teacher would have to negotiate his or her personal and religious beliefs with his or her professional role if he or she is to implement gay themes in the classroom (Goldstein, Collins, & Halder, 2007). Although some teachers may be hesitant, the more perseverant teachers could make the initial intent and this slowly may lead other teachers to follow suit.

Gay cultural proficiency training may help with the implementation of gay themes in the classroom by increasing awareness and knowledge among parents and teachers. Cultural proficiency is a step toward reaching empathy, understanding, and contact with gays and lesbians, as the contact theory hypothesis suggests (Overby & Barth 2002). Acceptance of others requires tolerance, sensitivity, and cultural awareness training (Goodenow, Szalacha, & Westheimer, 2006; Sogunro, 2001). Cultural proficiency training may also assist teachers with learning the facts about gays and dispel the myths and misconceptions, the reason for some of those feelings of discomfort (Solomon, 2004). Teachers could obtain the knowledge by taking courses at a local Gay and Lesbian Center or reading biographies about gay people, such as Harvey Milk or Bayard Rustin. Movies and documentaries are a great resource to learn about gay culture; however, teachers would need to take that initiative and be ready to deal with the cognitive dissonance and disequilibrium.

Another step toward having a more inclusive classroom curriculum would be to understand the goals and ideals of multicultural education. In order for multiculturalism to succeed, however, a teacher would need to renounce his or her prejudicial attitudes and negotiate his or her personal and religious beliefs with his or her professional role if he or she is to implement gay themes in the classroom as multicultural education (Goldstein et al., 2007).

Teachers should be aware that gay culture is part of the multicultural education agenda and that preventing homophobia and heterosexism is an essential element of the NAME (Holland, 2005; NAME, 2005a, 2005b). In addition, because some teachers and administrators do not accept gay culture as a culture, they must be instructed that cultural identity is defined as the self-perception of one's social positioning in life, such as race, social class, gender, religion, age, and sexual orientation, as well as physical and mental

22

ability (Chen, 2005). During my past trainings with staff and colleagues, some teachers had objected to gay culture being considered a culture. However, after discussing critical pedagogy, contact theory hypothesis, and NAME's goals, teachers became less resistant and began to listen and accept--and some to implement-- gay themes in the classroom.

Another important step would be to understand the purpose for implementing gay themes in the classroom. Multicultural education that includes discussions about sexual orientation focuses on discussions about issues associated with being gay and gay communities and cultures, including the themes of love, families, respect, and relationships (Swartz, 2003; Wolfe, 2006). The purpose of including gay-themed children's literature is to teach about diversity, tolerance, and acceptance of homosexuals and LGBT people (Athanases, 1996; Moita-Lopes, 2006; Swartz, 2003). Another reason for including gay themes is to provide a safer learning environment for all students, which this may lead to less bullying and negative playground chatter where one hears the derogatory phrase, "that's so gay."

Implementing gay themes in the elementary classroom as well as conducting professional development and training for teachers, the aforementioned steps were critical for successful implementation. Mentioning NAME's goals, district/school policy (if applicable), and the purpose for implementing gay themes in the classroom avoided disagreement and teachers became more focused on the training at hand. In all the years that I have been implementing gay themes in the elementary classroom, I have had about 2-3 parents complain to the principal and one teacher walk out of professional training. In the end, the training was successful and I realized it is fine for some to disagree.

Another step is for teachers to understand the purpose of gay-themed children's literature; the purpose specifically being to create a more diverse learning environment that welcomes gay families and their cultures. Because the children of gay parents consist of an estimated one million children in the United States (Peterschick-Gilmore & Bell, 2006) and the children of gay parents are often bullied, rejected, or harassed by their peers (Clarke, Kitzinger, & Potter, 2004), gay families and the children of gay families require representation and validation in schools and within

24

society through children's literature. Such representation may dispel misconceptions and help increase the self-esteem of children from gay families, thus improving the achievement levels of students in general.

Parents may be a possible reason for teachers excluding gay-themed children's literature from the classroom. As I discussed previously (Flores, 2009), some teachers have suggested in a study that parental concerns might be an obstacle to implementing gay-themed children's literature within multicultural education program. Schools and educational leaders must provide adequate support to teachers who implement gay themes in the classroom. Once teachers know that they have the support of their school district and administrators then implementation is more feasible. In addition, if district policy is enacted the case for parental objection becomes irrelevant.

However, in order to handle parental concerns, teachers would have to learn specifically about district policies toward implementing gay-themed children's literature as well as how to deal with parents' concerns and students' questions. Again, teachers need to focus on the inclusion of gay themes is to increase tolerance and create a safe learning environment for all students. If teachers and parents are informed of the purpose, the implementation of gay themes may be more feasible. In addition, it is important to mention that implementing gay themes or gay-themed children's literature does not involve discussions of sex or homosexual behavior; instead, the focus is on tolerance, familial diversity, love, and acceptance.

As an educator who has implemented gay themes in the elementary classroom, if there were parents who complained, my defense was NAME's goals and the district's inclusive multicultural education policy. The Los Angeles Unified School District (LAUSD) and Board officials emphasized that support for a teacher was unlimited in relation to the implementation of gay-themed literature in the classroom. The LAUSD and the Board of Education have adopted June as Gay and Lesbian Pride Month. LAUSD policy states the following, enacted in 1992:

> The Board of Education of the Los Angeles Unified School
> District hereby declares June as Gay and Lesbian Pride
> Month and directs the Superintendent and all District staff
> to support lessons and activities that engage students in

meaningful learning, research and writing about our lesbian, gay, bisexual, and transgender students and families.

Teachers need to know that they have the support of their school districts and administrative personnel. Likewise, it is essential that all stakeholders be informed about school district policies that approve diverse multicultural education materials that are inclusive of gay culture, gay themes, and gay-themed children's literature. If teachers are not aware of district policies about gay themes and tolerance education inclusion, district officials need to do more to make the policies visible through memorandums, e-mails, mailings, and newsletters.

However, some schools lack the services to protect and meet the needs of the LGBT students (Gay, Lesbian, and Straight Education Network [GLSEN], 2003), policy is important for the success of all students. If no clear policy exists, it is critical that policy be created to support teachers, parents, and students, including gay youth (Allan, 1999). Policy should provide support for teachers who intend to implement diverse multicultural themes that include gay themes and create an anti-violence/bully code for sexual minorities (Allan, 1999).

Creating and having policy is important because students who have appropriate representation and support at school tend to thrive within their educational environments (Hansman, 1998; Sogunro, 2001). Teachers and staff need to maintain a harassment-free, safe environment for gay youth because current laws and courts have addressed the issue of harassment of sexual minority students. Schools are liable if inaction and complacency to the needs of sexual minority students exist (National Center for Lesbian Rights, 2004); in that sense, policy may be more important than ever.

In order to implement gay themes and gay-themed children's literature successfully, another step would be teachers receiving pedagogical training. Teachers would require training in the area of sexuality, sexual orientation, and sexual diversity, with self-awareness being a critical element (Rienzo et al., 2006; Van Wormer & McKinney, 2003). In addition, teachers should have access to examples set by past teachers and how they have implemented gay themes in the classroom, for example the documentary *It's Elementary* (Chasnoff & Cohen, 1995).

The lessons I developed for my students were simple enough. I turned to widely read gay-themed children's books such as *And Tango Makes Three* (2005) and *Asha's Mums* (1990). These two books directly address nontraditional family structures and send the message that some families may look different from the nuclear family but still encompass as much love and care, as do the nuclear families. After each book was read and discussed, the children returned to their desks, wrote a summary, and drew an accompanying illustration. By the end of June, the students had about 14 different books within their "Tolerance Bibliography" dealing with subjects such as gay families, homelessness, immigration, and disabilities. The discussions were rich and enlightening. The children's literature helped build positive discussions, and children tend to respond very well to books and literature (Aronson, 2004; Wolfe, 2006). Teaching tolerance and acceptance through children's literature may help reduce intolerance and homophobic attitudes (Moita-Lopez, 2006; Swartz, 2003).

The following are some books I have used myself that are available to teachers: Edmonds' (2000) *Mama Eat Ant Yuck!,*

Kennedy's (1998) *Lucy Goes to the Country*, Newman's (1989) *Heather has Two Mommies*, Valentine's (2004) *One Dad, Two Dad, Brown Dad, Blue Dads*, Willhoite's (1991) *Daddy's Roommate*, and Richardson and Parnell's (2005) *And Tango Makes Three*.

Books available for older children include Bauer's (1994) *Am I Blue? Coming Out of the Silence*, Crutcher's (1995, 1991) adventure novels *Ironman* and *Athletic Shorts*, Haskins' (1997) biography of *Bayard Rustin*, Peter's (2004) novel *Luna*, and Kaeser's (1999) *Love Makes a Family* (Swartz, 2003). Visit the Welcoming Schools' web page for a more thorough bibliographical list of gay-themed children's literature:

http://www.welcomingschools.org/2012/03/bibliographies-books-to-engage-students/

Visit the GSA Network's web page to see LGBT-inclusive lessons and activities for your classroom: http://gsanetwork.org/fair

Nevertheless, one may still ask why teach children, especially young children, about gays and lesbians? Because of a child's psychosocial and cognitive developmental characteristics, early childhood and adolescence are appropriate times to introduce multicultural education topics. Young children and adolescents can profit from experiences that advocate positive feelings toward themselves, others, and life within a diverse society (Blackburn, 2005; Manning, 2000). Teaching tolerance and educating children about sexual orientation can never start too early (Lai, 2006; Roffman, 2001; Solomon, 2004; Wolfe, 2006; Woody, 2002) because the creation of a child's prejudicial attitudes usually occurs during a child's early years (Willis, 2004).

During their period of growth, children and adolescents are forming cultural identities, establishing friendships, and developing opinions and a sense of fairness and justice. Young adolescents are cognitively and psychologically capable of grasping and comprehending injustices, unfair treatment, family diversity, and pluralism (Manning, 2000; Schall & Kauffmann, 2003).

Teachers should be made aware that gay youth are considered an at-risk population (Skegg, 2005). The high risks are parental rejection; hate crimes, peer abuse, homelessness, dropping out, poor achievement, drug abuse, suicide, and prostitution among gay youth (Hansman, 1998; Lucas, 2004). Knowing about the aforementioned risks may prompt teachers to accept the implementation of gay themes in the classroom. This may create a safer learning environment, increase support for gay youth, and improve academic achievement for all youth. This knowledge may change some teachers' attitudes toward implementing gay-themed children's literature and increase validation and acknowledgement of gay culture and the implementation of gay themes in the classroom.

The following strategies may help teachers in creating a more inclusive multicultural education and a more welcoming classroom. Allan (1999) suggested teachers might reduce stereotyping and create an open environment for expression with the following strategies:

a) Become a faculty sponsor of LGBT/GSA club or support group;

b) Network and use literature to increase knowledge;

c) Support an open, trusting, and welcoming classroom;

d) Choose literature that avoids gay stereotypes;

e) Join GLSEN (Gay Lesbian Straight Education Network);

f) Use or display materials by gay authors and historical figures such a Harvey Milk; and

g) Post or create school or district's education code against violence.

Van Wormer and McKinney (2003) offered the following ideas for micro-revolutionary change in classrooms:

a) Support safe sex-ed and discourage high-risk behavior like self-mutilation and self-abuse;

b) Organize workshops about sexual orientation for school leaders, staff, and administrators;

c) Institute programs that prevent bullying;

d) Provide support for gay and lesbian youth;

e) Link gays, lesbians, and their families to community resources;

f) Maintain confidentiality and honesty;

g) Provide the library with useful information about homosexuality; and

h) Invite LGBT people to conduct classroom discussions.

Because children begin to construct their gender and racial identities by the age of three, Araujo and Strasser (2003) offered suggestions for dealing with differences and helping young children to become comfortable with diversity and tolerance education:

a) Clarify misconceptions immediately;

b) Respond promptly to children's concerns and questions;

c) Provide simple and honest answers;

d) Introduce diversity and differences through children's age appropriate books and literature;

e) Offer children real-life experiences with real people;

f) Acknowledge children's fears and misconceptions;

g) Model respectful behavior verbally and non-verbally; and

h) Be fair, honest, and acknowledge if you do not know an answer.

Not only can teachers make a difference but also school districts and administrators. A correlation between self-esteem and academic performance is apparent; if students are low in self-esteem and feel underrepresented by the dominant culture, low academic performance may be the consequence (Sogunro, 2001). To provide opportunities for identification, school districts need to provide curricular materials representing the diversity that exists in society by including gay cultures. School districts need to be mindful and ensure curriculum address the diversity of society when adopting new curriculum (Allan, 1999).

People have asked me, an educator who implements gay themes in the elementary classroom, "What is the biggest reward?" The rewards are watching children become more tolerant individuals, hearing the word *'gay'* used less in a derogatory manner, less bullying on the school playground, and most rewarding of all, is to watch the children no longer squirm or giggle when I used the word gay in a casual manner.

There also have been parents and students who have thanked me for teaching them about gay themes. A parent once came to me thanking me for opening the doors of communication with her daughter. Another student once thanked me because I had widened his world view about different cultures and peoples, while another student would go to subsequent teachers asking each one what gay themes he or she was going to implement in the classroom just as I had.

As an educator, I realize the crucial service I am providing to my students and school climate. I carry a message of tolerance and acceptance wherever I go. Gay themes in the classroom are very controversial; to some it is scary, and to others it is wrong. However, the reason gay themes should be implemented is to stop the prevalent hatred directed toward gays. Although the ideas may seem simplistic to some, we have to begin now and make micro-revolutionary changes to our curriculum and instruction. If no child is to be left behind, schools must provide safe, supportive learning environments for all youth, including gay youth, and start the change process today (Goodenow et al., 2006; Wolfe, 2006).

In conclusion, the aforementioned steps may serve to create a more inclusive multicultural education that includes gay themes. If school leadership, teachers, and parents validate and acknowledge gay cultures, tolerance is possible, and increased knowledge would reduce societal homophobia. Tolerance and decreased homophobia may increase student achievement and create a safer learning environment for all youth, including gay youth (Hansman, 1998; Swartz, 2003). Improved curriculum, proper training, and strong leadership skills will help to lessen problems that may surface during the implementation of gay-themed children's literature. With the cooperation of school districts, educational leaders, and all stakeholders, implementing gay-themed children's literature may be possible, and a brighter future for all youth may be on the horizon.

References

Allan, C. (1999). Poets of comrades: Addressing sexual orientation in the English classroom. *English Journal, 88*(6), 97.

Araujo, L., & Strasser, J. (2003). Confronting prejudice in the early childhood classroom. *Kappa Delta Pi Record, 39*(4), 178.

Aronson, M. (2004). How are children affected by the books in their lives? *World Literature Today, 78*(2), 14-15.

Athanases, S. Z. (1996). A gay-themed lesson in an ethnic literature curriculum: Tenth graders' response to "Dear Anita." *Harvard Educational Review, 66*(2), 231.

Barber, H., & Krane, V. (2007). Creating a positive climate for lesbian, gay, bisexual, and transgender youths. *Journal of Physical Education, Recreation, and Dance, 78*(7), 52.

Bassett, R. L., van Nikkelen-Kuyper, M., Johnson, D., Miller, A., Carter, A., & Grimm, J. P. (2005). Being a good neighbor: Can students come to value homosexual persons? *Journal of Psychology and Theology, 33*(1), 17.

Birden, S. (2002). Teaching with "attitude:" Coming to grips with the truths and consequences of ignoring sexual diversity in schools. *Educational Foundations, 16*(4), 53.

Blackburn, M. V. (2005). Teaching queer-inclusive language arts: The authors argue that because literature means more to readers when they see themselves in a story, queer-inclusive literature should be taught in schools. *Journal of Adolescents & Adult Literacy, 49*(3), 202.

Bowen, A. M., & Bourgeois, M. J. (2001). Attitudes toward lesbian, gay, and bisexual college students: The contribution of pluralistic ignorance, dynamic social impact, and contact theories. *Journal of American College Health, 50*(2).

Chasnoff, D., & Cohen, H. S. (1995). *It's Elementary: Talking about gay issues in school* [video]. San Francisco, CA: Women's Educational Media.

Chen, H. J. (2005). The rationale for critical pedagogy in facilitating cultural identity development. *Curriculum and Teaching Dialogue, 7*(1/2), 11-22.

Clarke, V., Kitzinger, C., & Potter, J. (2004). Kids are just cruel anyway: Lesbian and gay parents talk about homophobic bullying. *British Journal of Social Psychology, 43,* 531.

Cosier, K., & Sanders, J. H. (2007). Queering art teacher education. *International Journal of Art & Design Education, 26*(1), 21-30.

Crary, E. (1992). *Talking about differences children notice.* In B. Neugebauer, (Ed.), *Talking about differences children notice. In alike and different: Exploring our humanity with young children* (pp. 11-15). Washington, D.C.: National Association for the Education of Young Children.

Daniel, P. L. (2007). Invitation to all: Welcoming gays and lesbians into my classroom and curriculum. *English Journal, 96*(5), 75-80.

Flores, G. (2009). Teachers' attitudes in implementing gay-themed children's literature as part of a balanced multicultural education curriculum (Doctoral dissertation, University of Phoenix, 2009). (UMI Microform # 3370947).

Gay, Lesbian, and Straight Education Network [GLSEN]. (2003, December 8). *National school climate survey.* Retrieved from http://www.glsen.org /templates/news/record.html?section=13%26record=1656

Giugni, M., & Semann, A. (2004). It's elementary: Talking about gay issues in school [video]. *Teaching Education, 15*(1), 121-125.

Goldstein, T., Collins, A., & Halder, M. (2007). Anti-homophobia education in public schooling: A Canadian case study of policy implementation. *Journal of Gay & Lesbian Social Services, 19*(3/4), 47-66.

Goodenow, C., Szalacha, L., & Westheimer, K. (2006). School support groups, other school factors, and the safety of sexual minority adolescents. *Psychology in the Schools, 43*(5), 573-589.

Hansman, G. P. (1998). Multicultural education and queer youth. Montreal, Canada. Retrieved from http://www.youth.org/loco/PERSONProject /Resources /OrganizingResources/hansman.html

Hermann-Wilmarth, J. M. (2007). Full inclusion: Understanding the role of gay and lesbian texts and films in teacher education classrooms. *Language Arts, 84*(4), 347-356.

Holland, R. (2005). Multicultural educators: Disciples of social justice. *School Reform News.* Arlington: The Heartland Institute.

Lai, Y. C. (2006). A preliminary study of teachers' perceptions of sex education in Hong Kong Preschools. *Australian Journal of Early Childhood, 31*(3), 1.

Lucas, T. (2004). Homophobia: An issue for every pupil? *Education Review, 17*(2), 66-72.

Maher, M. J. (2007). Gay and lesbian students in Catholic high schools: A qualitative study of alumni narratives. *Catholic Education: A Journal of Inquiry & Practice, 10*(4), 449-472.

Manning, M. L. (2000). Developing responsive multicultural education for young adolescents. *Childhood Education, 76*(2), 82.

Milton, J. (2003). Primary school sex education programs: Views and experiences of teachers in four primary schools in Sydney, Australia. *Sex Education, 3*(3), 241-257.

Moita-Lopes, L. P. (2006). Queering literacy teaching: Analyzing gay-themed discourses in a fifth-grade class in Brazil. *Journal of Language, Identity, & Education, 5*(1), 31-50.

National Association of Multicultural Education [NAME]. (2005a). *National Association of Multicultural Education definition.* Retrieved from http://www.nameorg.org/resolutions/definition.html

National Association of Multicultural Education [NAME]. (2005b). Retrieved from www.nameorg.org

National Center for Lesbian Rights. (2004). *Harassment and discrimination: A legal overview.* San Francisco, CA: Author. Retrieved from http://nelrights.org/publications/pubs/ha-legaloverview0104.pdf

Overby, L. M., & Barth, J. (2002). Contact, community context and public attitudes toward gay men and lesbians. *Polity, 34*(4), 433.

Peterschick-Gilmore, D., & Bell, K. (2006). We are family: Using diverse family structure literature with children. *Reading Horizons, 46*(4), 279-299.

Rienzo, B. A., Button, J. W., Jiunn-Jye, S., & Ying, L. (2006). The politics of sexual orientation issues in American schools. *Journal of School Health, 76*(3), 93-97.

Roffman, D. M. (2001). *Sex and sensibility: The thinking parent's guide to talking sense about sex.* Cambridge, England: Perseus.

Satterly, B. A., & Dyson, D. A. (2005). Educating all children equitably: A strengths-based approach to advocacy for sexual minority youth in schools. *Contemporary Sexuality, 39*(3), i-viii.

Schall, J., & Kauffmann, G. (2003). Exploring literature with gay and lesbian characters in the elementary school. *Journal of Children's Literature, 29*(1), 36-45.

Skegg, K. (2005, October). Seminar one: Self-harm. *Lancet, 366*, 1471.

Sogunro, O. A. (2001). Toward multiculturalism: Implications of multicultural education for schools. *Multicultural Perspectives, 3*(3), 19.

Solomon, S. (2004). Kids say the funniest things . . . Anti-homophobia group work in the classroom. *Teaching Education, 15*(1), 103-106.

Swartz, P. C. (2003). Bridging multicultural education: Bringing sexual orientation into the children's and young adult literature classrooms. *Radical Teacher, 66*, 11.

Van Wormer, K., & McKinney, R. (2003). What schools can do to help gay/lesbian youth: A harm reduction approach. *Adolescence, 38*(151), 409.

Ventura, L. A., Lambert, E. G., Bryant, M., & Pasupuleti, S. (2004). Differences in attitudes toward gays and lesbians among criminal justice and non-criminal justice majors. *American Journal of Criminal Justice, 28*(2), 165.

Willis, D. G. (2004). Hate crimes against gay males: An overview. *Issues in Mental Health Nursing, 25*, 115.

Wolfe, R. B. (2006). Choosing to include gay issues in early childhood teacher preparation coursework: One professor's journey. *Journal of Early Childhood Teacher Education, 27*(2), 195-204.

Woody, J. D. (2002). *How can we talk about that? Overcoming personal hang-ups so we can teach kids the right stuff about sex and morality*. San Francisco, CA: Jossey-Bass.

3 The New Entrepreneur
J. Phillip Harris

Winston Churchill (Churchill, n.d.) once said, "Success is walking from failure to failure with no loss of enthusiasm." The new entrepreneur walks a tightrope in the emerging global market where government favors monopolies, but society needs the innovation, growth, and jobs entrepreneurs create. A gap exists in the global economy because government and big business have a vacuum in leadership to deal with social issues (Soros, 1998). Entrepreneurial fortitude can deal with constant barriers and break them down one at a time. Entrepreneurs can convert the corruption, greed, and self-interest in government and large companies into a more appealing economic system by listening to people and consumers' needs. Without entrepreneurship, leadership fails because of a breakdown in trust. Entrepreneurs can attract capital to innovative ideas in response to consumer needs taking the pulse of the people. The entrepreneur is an agile force where gridlock prevails. Consumers and workers yearn for the leadership only an entrepreneur can provide to guide them through the 21st century. Society craves leadership it can trust and does not want government and business to talk down to people depicting them as second-class citizens. People long for the leader who unites rather than divides. People want to believe in a cause and a dream, not narrow motives increasing the wealth of the elite. I aim at addressing the role of the 21st century entrepreneur in the new global society measured against the views of the entrepreneur in earlier societies.

Review of the Literature

Long (1983) noted that redefining entrepreneurship should not remove ambiguities in its definition, but stress its continuing value. Cantillon (1755) described entrepreneurs as people who are adventurers or undertakers. Cantillon further portrays the entrepreneur as self-employed and confronted by uncertain conditions. Cantillon considered the entrepreneur clever and knowledgeable. Praag (1999) claimed the entrepreneur also has responsibility for bringing supply and demand into equilibrium.

Expanding on the Cantillon (1755) view, Say (1847) reasoned entrepreneurs gain capital by making the right contacts. The seasoned entrepreneur has the right combination of moral qualities

and world knowledge. Entrepreneurs precisely estimate the

demand for critical products. Similarly, the entrepreneur organizes

labor, raw materials, and finds consumers for these products. Say

added the entrepreneur overcomes notable obstacles.

Entrepreneurs to succeed must have managerial talent (Cantillon,

1755; Long, 1983; Say, 1847). Praag (1999) noted according to Say's

theory of production, distribution, and consumption, the

entrepreneur is both a leader and a manager having unique

qualities and experience.

Marshall (1961) took a similar view arguing that

entrepreneurs must have managerial talent. Marshall claimed

entrepreneurs must have administrative skills with the ability to

innovate. Marshall aided in the birth of the corporate

organizational form. Similarly, Marshall championed the influence

offered by the corporate organizational form. The Marshallian

challenge stemmed from separating ownership and management.

Marshall believed the owners should bear the risk, while the

managers should control the organization (Marshall, 1961;

Zaratiegui & Rabade, 2005). According to Praag (1999), Marshall believed entrepreneurs creating innovations need certain skills to award benefits on society.

Schumpeter (1994) took another view of the entrepreneur, and espoused the main role of the entrepreneur is to create. Schumpeter coined the term "creative destruction," and forecast bureaucratic business managers would overtake ingenious entrepreneurs creating anti-capitalistic conditions and foster socialism (p. 70). Socialism in Schumpeter's view benefited corrupt society. Schumpeter looked at "creative destruction" as a series of actions instead of a static condition, and suggested imaginative entrepreneurs would resurface to replace socialism with capitalism (p. 70). Skousen (2008), for example, noted Microsoft overtaking a corporate mammoth like International Business Machines would not have surprised Schumpeter.

Apart from the Austrian school, Knight (1921) fathered the Chicago school of economics. Similar to Cantillon's (1755) view of entrepreneurs as adventurers, Knight's key contribution distinguished risk from uncertainty. Knight defined risk as conditions with knowable chances of happening. Knight reduces uncertainty to unknown conditions for which one cannot estimate the chance of happening. Knight believed entrepreneurs' role is to face uncertain conditions, and entrepreneurs must have administrative competence because they share in the managerial roles. Unlike Cantillon, Knight did not believe achieving equilibrium conditions is a role of the entrepreneur (Knight, 1921; Long, 1983).

Leibenstein (1979) backed Knight's view the entrepreneur needs managerial skills. Leibenstein added the entrepreneur's role is to reduce organizational inefficiency. Leibenstein argued the entrepreneur reverses organizational decline through introducing new efficiencies.

Montanye (2006) viewed the entrepreneur as "a mildly heroic figure" (p. 548). Austrian economist, Mises (1944) believed that entrepreneurs serve consumers by seeing existing goods and services as they are and making them better. The entrepreneur works in society's interest by considering consumers' needs. Mises added the entrepreneur is a speculator who deals with unknown and uncertain conditions to better society. The entrepreneur foresees what benefits consumers and works tirelessly to perfect goods and services meeting this goal. Mises distinguished the entrepreneur from corporate managers. Corporate managers to Mises are subservient to entrepreneurs. Corporate managers are merely promoters benefiting from superior information to profit for their own self-interest, but cannot replace the dedication by entrepreneurs to special interests of the consumer (Mises, 1944; Montanye, 2006).

Although Mises (1944) viewed the entrepreneur as indispensable, Coase (1937) believed the entrepreneur is replaceable and does not add any value. Coase argued the entrepreneur adds transaction costs, which monopolies can remove by becoming more efficient. Leibenstein (1983) challenged Coase's argument noting that monopolies do not remove the transaction costs, which entrepreneurs add, but simply replace them within the firm. Coase's argument fails to consider most monopolies are not efficient because of the lack of competition. Smith's (1976, 1980) vision of free markets feared monopolies because shielding firms from having to compete is counter to competition that drives efficiency (Bassiry & Jones, 1993). Louis D. Brandeis, one of the most celebrated Chief Justices in United States history, defended efforts opposing corporate bigness because he believed it detracted from market efficiency (Savino, 2009). According to Skousen (2008), Mises believed capitalism would unseat the eventual collapse of socialism making clear Schumpeter's belief in entrepreneurship going through different cycles. In harmony with Schumpeter's "creative destruction" idea (Schumpeter, 1994, p. 70), Baumol (1990) showed how historically entrepreneurs went through industrious and disparaging cycles.

Contrary to Smith, Baumol, and Brandeis (Bassiry & Jones, 1993; Baumol, Litan, & Schramm, 2007; Brandeis, 1934), Kirzner (1999) believed entrepreneurs seek pure profit and the absence of government intervention. Kirzner's main line of reasoning is entrepreneurs rely on superior information to take advantage of arbitrage opportunities. Unlike Mises (1944) and Schumpeter (1994) whom credited superior information to the corporate manager, Kirzner credited this information to the entrepreneur. Kirzner believed superior information suited the self-interest of the entrepreneur.

How the Entrepreneur Has Changed

Surely, the entrepreneur today shares many of these characteristics. Soros (1998) described a global open society as a place in which a free flow of capital and ideas exists. According to Soros, the global open society faces five major problems. First, an uneven distribution of benefits exists because capital is more mobile than labor. Another problem experienced is unstable international financial markets unresponsive to market expectations and supply and demand. A larger problem stems from the threat of monopolies and oligopolies erasing competition because of deregulation. This concentration of power undermines the state from protecting the welfare of citizens. Last, and most important, no glue exists to preserve and protect social values and cohesion of diverse nations.

Despite an uneven distribution of benefits in an open global society, capital will flow where creativity and innovation exists. The entrepreneur has a major role in attracting capital for innovative new ideas. A nation should promote entrepreneurship despite pressure from large companies seeing competition as a threat. Honig and Dana (2008) highlighted the devastating effects on communities without entrepreneurship.

Unstable international financial markets mainly affect entrepreneurs by not working toward market equilibrium and stymieing entrepreneurs' efforts to fill gaps in the market. Usually, supply and demand fills market gaps because entrepreneurs find and take advantage of unexploited opportunities. Large global firms ration supply by keeping prices high on existing goods and services and not finding novel solutions to supply and demand gaps (Soros, 2008). Entrepreneurs play a critical role in finding these gaps. However, entrepreneurs rely on supply and demand and the forces of equilibrium to fill market gaps. The international entrepreneur must protect novel and creative solutions from monopolies and oligopolies wishing to take advantage of them. Monopolies and oligopolies lessen entrepreneurs' ability to compete; without any rule of law, these companies remove competition, causing gaps in supply and demand (Soros, 2008). These conditions put entrepreneurs in a hostile environment. The global entrepreneur is more apt to survive by networking and working through channel partners to avoid falling prey to these monopolies.

Although Soros (2008) argued this buildup of power endangers nation-states from protecting the welfare of the people, the entrepreneur has to find ways to satisfy the values of the citizenry. Filling this gap better equips the entrepreneurs rather than large companies to understand citizens' values and target goods and services to their values. Governments should respond to the needs of citizens in democratic society. Ironically, the editors of the *Monthly Review* credited the Occupy Movements to unfinished business from the time of Lincoln, the first Republican President. President Lincoln envisaged labor as the true source of value over capital. Lincoln championed worker rights avoiding conditions of slavery (Huberman, Foster, Sweezy, & Magdoff, 2011). Entrepreneurs offer a way to address citizens' needs, which is another reason entrepreneurs are critical. The state has a responsibility to the people, not large multinational companies.

Some of the skills credited to the global entrepreneur in the 21st century include the ability to network effectively, put creation before profit, and genuinely find ways to improve people's lives. For example, Levy (2011) explained Steve Jobs left Apple when the company took the focus off the product and put it instead on shareholder wealth maximization. Jobs showed a fanaticism for perfecting the product to his utter satisfaction. Entrepreneurs must act not solely for profit, but satisfy the interest of people they serve. Jobs loved helping people and envisaged their needs.

Multinational companies manage uncertainty and risk with predictive logic through planning efforts. Experienced entrepreneurs manage uncertainty much differently. The modern entrepreneur uses effectuation to take small trial and error steps reducing the risk of loss from uncertain conditions (Dew, Read, Sarasvathy, & Wiltbank, 2009; Read, Dew, Sarasvathy, Song, & Wiltbank, 2009; Sarasvathy & Dew, 2003). The modern entrepreneur leads into the future using the effectual methods, whereas multinational companies plan for what they know and avoid what they do not know.

Large companies are more likely to fall to Schumpeter's (1994) "creative destruction," which destroys human values without the influence of the entrepreneur (p. 70). Today's entrepreneurs provide the creativity needed to temper this series of actions.

The Role of Leadership

Executive expertise is also widely discussed by economic scholars, but today leadership has eclipsed executive skills as a major characteristic. Today's entrepreneurs not only must have administrative competence, but also gain the confidence of workers by building trust. A leader builds trust by working as a mentor and guide to workers instead of a command-and-control type manager. Besides having administrative skills, modern entrepreneurs must build the confidence of the workforce.

Darling and Beebe (2007) found four key leadership approaches for entrepreneurs. First, the entrepreneur gains attention through vision. The entrepreneurial leader crafts the future from the unknown. Second, a firm finds meaning through communication. Superior performance depends on stellar communication. Third, the founder must garner trust through positioning the firm. The entrepreneurial leader develops committed employees by entrusting them. By building integrity the leader gains the trust of the workers. Last, a leader gains respect from displaying confidence. A confident leader helps others achieve success.

Innovation is another reason an entrepreneurial leader needs to build trust. Dovey (2009) found innovation depends on social capital. Entrepreneurs must have the ability to foster trust in social networks and extend trust beyond the internal organization. An

54

entrepreneurial leader must build an administrative arrangement aligning with channel partners so it can compete in an ingenious way. Bowerman (2003) argued a firm fostering action learning helps make known guidelines to managers necessary for building inventive solutions in the business.

Educational Implications

Entrepreneurial leaders need to learn more about leadership approaches than about planning. Although the leader still needs good business skills, the entrepreneurial leader relies more on an adhocracy culture to entrust workers. An adhocracy culture promotes risk taking, alignment with vision, and innovation, while holding the organization with active learning (Masood, Dani, Burns, & Backhouse, 2006; Mintzberg, 1980). Learning is more important on-the- job than in a classroom highlighting business planning skills.

Another feature of the learning environment is a culture promoting freedom and agility to try new approaches. The entrepreneurial leader must listen and show compassion promoting leader-follower relations. Good leadership demands a more servant-leadership style. The entrepreneurial leaders should have charismatic characteristics coupled with good citizenship (Abbasi, Siddiqi, & Azim, 2011; Joseph & Winston, 2005).

Apart from on-the-job education, good entrepreneurial education programs need to offer a blend between experience and classroom learning. Although normal classroom approaches stress skills entrepreneurs need, practical application is necessary. Practical experience fosters creativity and learning about entrepreneurial behavior. A recent study showed students can improve understanding about entrepreneurship, leadership, self-esteem, team skills, and communication skills through a trial program blending experience and classroom learning. A blended program offers students and their mentors a chance to reflect on their experiences to improve (Hernandez & Newman, 2006).

Conclusion

Global markets have produced a gap only the entrepreneur can fill. The new entrepreneur fills market gaps unfulfilled by large companies and keeps markets efficient and responsive to people's needs. The new entrepreneur leads change in unexplored territory by nimbly taking advantage of opportunities despite having to overcome obstacles created by big business and government attempts to thwart competition. Another key role of the new

entrepreneur is to moderate conditions leading to "creative

destruction" (Schumpeter, 1994, p.70) and the devastating effects on

communities without entrepreneurship. The new entrepreneur

combines leadership and management skills. Today's entrepreneur

must have a vision and entrust employees to work toward

satisfying unexploited gaps in the market and build the trust of

consumers. The new entrepreneur must put perfection of products

and services to fill these gaps ahead of pure profit. In this search for

perfection, the new entrepreneur values people both in the form of

employees and consumers. Servant leadership helps the new

entrepreneur guide people toward a common mission. The new

entrepreneur serves as the voice of the people in a corrupt and

broken political setting filled with greed and gridlock. Education

plays an important role for the new entrepreneur, but needs more

learning from experiences on-the-job. The new entrepreneur

develops skills by doing rather than excessively planning.

References

Abbasi, M. H., Siddiqi, A., & Azim, R. U. A. (2011). Role of effective communications for enhancing leadership and entrepreneurial skills in university students. *International Journal of Business & Social Science, 2*(10), 242-250.

Bassiry, G. R., & Jones, M. (1993). Adam Smith and the ethics of contemporary capitalism. *Journal of Business Ethics, 12*(8), 621.

Baumol, W. J. (1990). Entrepreneurship: Productive, unproductive, and destructive. *Journal of Political Economy, 98*(5), 893-921. doi: 10.1086/261712

Baumol, W. J., Litan, R. E., & Schramm, C. J. (2007). *Good capitalism, bad capitalism and economics of growth and prosperity.* New Haven, Conn. and London, England: Yale University Press.

Bowerman, J. K. (2003). Leadership development through action learning: An executive monograph. *Leadership in Health Services, 16*(4), 6-14. doi: 10.1108/13660750310500049

Brandeis, L. D. (1934). *The curse of bigness: Miscellaneous papers of Louis D. Brandeis.* New York, NY: Viking Press.

Cantillon, R. (1755). *Essai sur la nature du commerce en general.* London.

Churchill, W. (n.d.). 99 inspirational & motivational quotes on entrepreneurship. Retrieved from http://www.minterest.com/99-inspirational-motivational-quotes-on-entrepreneurship/

Coase, R. H. (1937). The nature of the firm. *Economica, 4*(16), 386-405. doi: 10.1111/j.1468-0335.1937.tb00002.x

Darling, J. R., & Beebe, S. A. (2007). Effective entrepreneurial communication in organization development: Achieving excellence based on leadership strategies and values. *Organization Development Journal, 25*(1), 76-93.

Dew, N., Read, S., Sarasvathy, S. D., & Wiltbank, R. (2009). Effectual versus predictive logics in entrepreneurial decision-making: Differences between experts and novices. *Journal of Business Venturing, 24*(4), 287-309. doi: 10.1016/j.jbusvent.2008.02.002

Dovey, K. (2009). The role of trust in innovation. *The Learning Organization, 16*(4), 311-325. doi: 10.1108/09696470910960400

Hernandez, S. A., & Newman, C. M. (2006). Minding our business: A model of service-learning in entrepreneurship education. *Journal of Entrepreneurship Education, 9*(10988394), 53-75. Retrieved from http://www.alliedacademies.org/Publications/Papers/JEE%20Vol%209%202006%20p%2053-75.pdf

Honig, B., & Dana, L. P. (2008). Communities of disentrepreneurship. *Journal of Enterprising Communities: People and Places in the Global Economy, 2*(1), 5-20. doi: 10.1108/17506200810861221

Huberman, L., Foster, J. B., Sweezy, P., & Magdoff, H. (2011). Notes from the editors. *Monthly Review: An Independent Socialist Magazine, 63*(7), 62-64.

Joseph, E. E., & Winston, B. E. (2005). A correlation of servant leadership, leader trust, and organizational trust. *Leadership & Organization Development Journal, 26*(1), 6-22. doi: 10.1108/01437730510575552

Kirzner, I. M. (1999). Mises and his understanding of the capitalist system *CATO Journal, 19*(2), 215.

Knight, F. H. (1921). *Risk, uncertainty, and profit* (2002 Reprint ed.). Washington, DC: Beard Books.

Leibenstein, H. (1979). The general x-efficiency paradigm and the role of the entrepreneur. In M. J. Rizzo (Ed.), *Time, Uncertainty and Disequilibrium* (pp. 127-139). Lexington, Mass.: Lexington Books.

Leibenstein, H. (1983). Property rights and x-efficiency: Comment, *American Economic Review*, p. 831.

Levy, S. (2011). The revolution according to Steve Jobs. *Wired*. Retrieved from http://www.wired.com/magazine/2011/11/ff_stevejobs/all/1

Long, W. (1983). The meaning of entrepreneurship. *American Journal of Small Business, 8*(2), 47-56.

Marshall, A. (1961). *Principles of economics* (8th ed.). London, England: Macmillan.

Masood, S., Dani, S., Burns, N., & Backhouse, C. (2006). Transformational leadership and organizational culture: The situational strength perspective. *Proceedings of the Institution of Mechanical Engineers -- Part B -- Engineering Manufacture, 220*(6), 941-949. doi: 10.1243/09544054JEM499

Mintzberg, H. (1980). Structure in 5's: A synthesis of the research organization design. *Management Science, 26*(3), 322-341. doi: 0825-1909/80/2603/0323^1.25

von Mises, L. (1944). *Bureaucracy.* New Haven, Conn.: Yale University Press.

Montanye, J. A. (2006). Entrepreneurship. *Independent Review, 10*(4), 547.

van Praag, C. M. v. (1999). Some classic views on entrepreneurship. *De Economist, 147*(3), 311-311.

Read, S., Dew, N., Sarasvathy, S. D., Song, M., & Wiltbank, R. (2009). Marketing under uncertainty: The logic of an effectual approach. *Journal of Marketing, 73*(3), 1-18. doi: 10.1509/jmkg.73.3.1

Sarasvathy, S. D., & Dew, N. (2003, August). *Effectual networks: A pre-commitment approach to bridging the gap between opportunism and trust.* Paper presented at the In Organization and Managment Theory: Conference Paper Abstracts. Academy of Management Proceedings.

Savino, D. (2009). Louis D. Brandeis and his role promoting scientific management as a progressive movement. *Journal of Management History, 15*(1), 38-49. doi: 10.1108/17511340910921772

Say, J. B. (1847). *A treatise on political economy:* Grigg, Elliot & Co.

Schumpeter, J. A. (1994). *Capitalism, Socialism, and Democracy.* London, England: Routledge.

Skousen, M. (2008). *The making of modern economics: The lives and ideas of the great thinkers* (2nd ed.). Armonk, NY: M. E. Sharpe, Inc.

Smith, A. (1976). *An inquiry into the nature and causes of the wealth of nations.* Oxford, England: Clarendon Press.

Smith, A. (1980). *The wealth of nations.* New York, NY: Penquin Books.

Soros, G. (1998). Toward a global open society. *The Atlantic Online,*
281(1), 20-32. Retrieved from
http://www.theatlantic.com/past/docs/issues/98jan/open
soc.htm

Zaratiegui, J. M., & Rabade, L. A. (2005). Capital owners,
entrepreneurs and managers: A Marshallian scheme.
Management Decision, 43(5/6), 772-785. doi:
10.1108/00251740510597770

4 Leadership: Path or Destination
Frederick Littles

The researcher draws on subtleties between path (course of action) and destination (place of purpose) to discover the identity of leadership, an elusive phenomenon that has elected to embark on a journey of ambiguity. Jago (1982) posits that theorists, scholars, leaders, managers, and prominent societies have constructed the concept of a default identity of leadership as a never-ending process based on experiences, preparation, education, and self-study. Burns (1978) conveyed that leadership is instilled in an individual over time; it is not received at the time of birth. This takes the literature back to the question, is leadership defined as a path or destination? To provide a definitive argument for both topics, destination is a place to which one is often directed or guided. It offers a beginning and end. If leadership is based off of Burns's convictions, leadership never had a beginning since one knows the beginning of one's life is birth. Exploring the subtleties between path and leadership, it becomes clear that each is shaped by the other in subtle and explicit ways. The article takes a deeper look at leadership based on both path and destination.

Leadership

Leadership possesses clarity of vision, a sense of need that demonstrates the convictions and beliefs that allow individuals to make and take necessary risks. The true form of leadership wins both the hearts and minds of the people, thus creating a transformational process to transcend the complexities of leadership. Weiss (2005) argues leadership involves the complexities and eccentricities of the people, which require understanding motivation and leadership responsibility. Consequently, the development of humans has created increasingly challenging problems and needs, thus complex forms of theoretical approaches and leadership theories must emerge to address the ever-evolving issues faced among today's societies. The leader's essential deed is to encourage societies to be cognizant or aware of what define their ideologies so profoundly (Burns, 1978).

Defining leadership allows one to seek out their own interests, such as leadership styles, emerging leadership practices, ethical standards on a local and global basis, and the significance of applying learning models. The business world is rapidly changing; leaders need to focus more on leadership for providing a calm and optimistic view, through efforts of collaboration (Li & Hung, 2009). The goal of leadership is to create a supportive environment in which people can grow, thrive, and live within a society of revolving leadership.

Leadership thrives on developing plan of action to build a followership base. Leaders who have that 'awe' effect will most likely garner attention needed to build a followers base. Leaders look to foster growth, whereas, followers look to build upon the inspiration given by leadership. Wren (1995) suggests, transformational leaders must be envisioning, energizing, and enabling. Thus, garnering these leadership traits will enable leaders the opportunity to foster growth needed to improve organizational effectiveness.

As a leader, one should look to provide a positive environment, which allows others to become actively engaged in the learning process. Leaders must learn to collaborate with peers to enhance the instructional environment. Moreover, leaders eventually will become scholars, practitioners, and leaders within the educational community and within one's respective careers. These organizations will look to these newly found leaders for inspiration and guidance for a sense of direction.

In order for leadership to capitalize on such strengths and reduce weaknesses, one must learn to identify self. Sessa (2002) states, "there is no simple formula for leadership, leaders must find their own individuality of understanding one's own strengths and weaknesses" (p. 1027). Leaders should prepare for situations at all levels. Embracing leadership challenges will allow individuals to focus and apply strengths to face the challenges with a positive, rather than a negative attitude.

Leadership Traits

Leadership is approachable in several ways. To grasp the effectiveness or ineffectiveness of leaders, Wren (1995) suggests that the mental testing movement encouraged researchers to implement "personality tests" in search of the leadership trait. Clawson (2006) suggests the trait approach represents the earliest study of leadership; emphasizing the personal traits of leaders possessed an innate characteristic that generally depicted the amount of leadership qualities instilled in individuals from one another. The testing allows researchers the opportunity to seek out a set of characteristics shared by leaders, thus known as the trait approach.

The trait approach was the beginning of the dissection of leadership to understand the relevancy of leadership. Oyinlade (2006) reflection on the methods of assessing leadership effectiveness, suggests the effectiveness of a leader's potential is often difficult to assess. The basis of the trait approach will determine and define certain characteristic traits that will separate successfully individuals from others within the group. However, no definite trait can foretell who will become a leader. Traits do however play a role in leadership in numerous aspects (Nahavandi, 2006).

Traits alone do not identify leadership. To believe that traits alone identify leadership skills and qualities creates false assumptions. The complexity of leadership is too ambiguous to align certain traits to certain leadership styles. Leadership must underline a significant direction and guidance for an individual to reach the proper level of productivity. One must define his or her path first, before reaching a point of destination. Defining leadership as a path or destination allows an individual the opportunity to understand and reflect upon the roles of traits in leadership (Nahavandi, 2006). Consequently, traits are not enough to determine the core of true leadership; on the contrary, traits are factors that pave the way to assess the pre-conditions for effective leadership. Dubrin (2001) notes in order for an individual to develop a path to leadership one must possess eight distinctive traits: self-confidence, trustworthiness, assertiveness, emotional stability, sense-of-humor, self-awareness, cognitive skills, and emotional intelligence (p. 156).

These eight leadership traits form the basis of one's path, defining one's purpose to embark on a journey that will lead to a likely destination. One often speaks of a path as traveling from point A to point B, traveling with purpose utilizing necessary traits to define one's true purpose. Moreover, leadership traits allow one to define one's own philosophy. Defining leadership provides a potential blueprint of one's life, thus providing a positive impact for one's ambitions and personal desires. However, life is about finding one's own meaning and purpose for living. Baggini (2004) states, "the search for meaning is essentially personal" (p. 4). This approach allows an individual to seek a course of action, defining leadership as a path or destination, maybe both.

Leadership: A Course of Action

A central conviction I have held about leadership is that leadership is the path set in motion, actions that empower individuals toward a common purpose or vision. Hickman (2009) states leadership is shaping the opportunity into reality. Showcasing leadership does not necessarily mean that an individual has to be put in charge of others. Leadership can showcase one's personal growth. During one's lifetime most will come to understand one's own blueprint to personal growth. Corey and Corey (2010) noted a question one should ask oneself, "Where can I go from here?" To answer such a question, one must come to understand a sense of self. This brings us back to defining our own path or destination.

As one seeks the path of personal growth, experiences teach one to follow a path of realization. Often we must learn from painful experiences. The journey of life is not an easy transition. Individuals will experience trials and tribulations. Thus, one may feel a sense of enlightenment. According to King (2009), "enlightenment means the end of suffering, living above thought, being free of one's mind, and not creating anymore suffering for one's self and others" (p. 98). The goal one sets forth is creating a lasting abundance in one's life. Moreover, this path defines one's destination of purpose and discovery, developing unique ideas through leadership.

Path to Destination: The Importance of Embarking

The road to defining leadership is an ambiguous process; it is not always a straight path and never quite leads to one's choice of destination. Choices have taken many down the wrong road, yet one continues to take different paths. It is a fact that many of us get lost; what matters is that we decided to embark on an unknown journey. Leadership is about making the choice to do the unthinkable, sometimes without a plan. Leadership involves constructing a comprehensive and deeper aptitude for direction that goes beyond one's own destination. Each leadership journey is unique. There is no set path to the pinnacle of the leadership echelon within a respective organization. Moreover, when one speaks of such a journey in the sense of leadership, the destination often begins and ends. Consequently, without a path there cannot be a destination to begin with. Weiss (2005) argues leadership involves the complexities and eccentricities of people and requires understanding motivation and leadership responsibility. Leadership crafts desire and willpower to inspire others to achieve a common purpose.

Burns (1978) often conveyed that leadership is instilled in an individual over time; it is not received at the time of birth. This takes the research back to the question at hand: Is leadership defined as a path or a destination? To provide a definitive argument for both ideas, destination is a place to which one is often directed or guided. It offers a beginning and an end. If leadership is based on Burns's convictions, leadership never had a beginning because one knows the beginning of one's life is birth. The idea behind destination is the purpose of its intent. Moreover, the research investigates whether leadership is defined as a path, a conduit of purpose on which an individual may travel. Based on these two significant parallels, one can see the difficult task of defining leadership and solving the complexity many have faced throughout the years.

Many of us have bought puzzle books that require us to complete a maze, a game in which one enter into a specific place (Point A) while trying to reach the end of the maze itself (Point B). *Figure 1* depicts a self-drawn maze that reflects on a systematic process that established a beginning and end. Defining leadership allows us to define and reflect on one's own beginning and end. This labyrinth showcases that leadership starts with an individual but touches the masses. One cannot reach a destination without taking a step forward while entering into unknown territories.

PATH
POINT A

DESTINATION
POINT B

Figure 1. Depicts self-drawn maze

Conclusion

In conclusion, the characterizations of leadership will always remain elusive, yet the dissection of leadership will continue to be an ambiguous process. The subtleties between path (course of action) and destination (place of purpose) show a parallel that has elected to embark on a journey of ambiguity. Leadership could be defined as path or destination because one cannot co-exist without the other. A definitive argument has been made; destination is a place to which one is often directed or guided. It offers a path and end. Leadership is defined as an indefinable irony, a place of both ambiguity and knowledge.

References

Baggini, J. (2004). *What's it all about? Philosophy and the meaning of life*. New York, NY: Oxford University Press.

Burns, J. M. (1978) *Leadership*. New York, NY: Harper Collins.

Clawson, J. G. (2006). *Level three leadership: Getting below the surface*. (3rd ed.). Upper Saddle River, NJ: Pearson.

Corey, G. & Corey, M.S. (2010). *I never knew I had a choice: Explorations in personal growth*. Belmont, CA: Brooks/Cole.

Dubrin, A.J. (2001). *Human relations: Interpersonal job-oriented skills* (7th ed.). Upper Saddle River, NJ: Prentice Hall.

Hickman, G. H. (2009). *Leading organizations: Perspectives for a new era*. Thousand Oaks, CA: Sage Publications, Inc.

Jago, A. G. (1982). Leadership: Perspectives in theory and research. *Management Science, 28*(3), 315-336.

King, J. D. (2009). *World transformation: A guide to personal growth and consciousness*. Bloomington, IN: AuthorHouse.

Li, C., & Hung, C. (2009). The influence of transformational leadership on workplace relationships and job performance. *Social Behavior & Personality: An International Journal, 37*(8), 1129-1142.

Nahavandi, A. (2006). *The art and science of leadership* (4th ed.). Upper Saddle River, NJ: Pearson.

Oyinlade, A. O. (2006). A method of assessing leadership effectiveness: Introducing the essential behavioral leadership qualities approach. *Performance Improvement Quarterly, 19*(1), 25-40. doi: 1039250811.

Sessa, V. (2002). Leadership development: Paths to self-insight and professional growth. *Personnel Psychology, 55*(4), 1027-1030.

Weiss, W. H. (2005). Leadership. *Supervision, 66*(10), 17.

Wren, J. T. (1995). *The leader's companion: Insights on leadership through the ages*. New York, NY: The Free Press.

5 Effective Leadership: The Communication Angle
Edric Spruill

The term *effective leadership* can be very misleading and quite subjective. There are a myriad of variables that affect effective leadership such as organizational culture, organizational climate, the leader's capabilities, and a variety of other intangibles. However, one of the most rudimentary and often overlooked skills an effective leader should have is the ability to communicate well. In fact, this skill is so often overlooked that Crainer and Dearlove (2008) posit that when it comes to communication, leaders are scarcely educated on the subtleties of the true definition.

Today's leader has many ways of communicating: E-mail, BlackBerry, cell phone, landline telephone, and a variety of other mechanisms, but none of these media are beneficial unless the leader is acutely skilled in the art of communication. A leader cannot become most effective if the communication process is broken. A leader can strategize and plan however, if they are poor communicators nothing will ever be accomplished. According to Crainer and Dearlove (2008), in order to execute anything, the leader has to understand that communication lies at the foundation of the leadership process. Communication can be considered one of the core fundamentals of effective leadership.

It is believed that communication is easy for leaders (Baldoni, 2004) as there is a misconception that speaking is communicating. Speaking is not the same as communicating as speaking can be a unidirectional process wherein communication involves giving and receiving; this can be verbal and non-verbal. Baldoni posits, "communication is a two-way process that involves speaking and listening as well as checking for understanding" (p. 20). It is through this process that the leader is actually engaged in a communication process. The leader is using the most important leadership skill that ultimately determines if organizational goals and objectives are executed properly.

In this time of social media, dispersed work teams, modern technology, and a trend toward decentralized organizational structures, the communication gap has broadened tremendously. Leaders have to become more adept in understanding how to send and receive information using a myriad of technological pathways sometimes without the luxury of face-to-face communication. Due to these differing methods of communication, the process of effective communication has broken down. McFarlane (2010) aptly states "communication in our modern technologically fast-paced society suffers from 'social myopia' because individuals now desire fast and brief communication with less emphasis placed on appropriateness in linguistic forms, respectful and orderly expressions, and quality effectiveness..."(p. 2). Unfortunately this speed-and-action trap is what leaders become entangled within, instead of taking the necessary time to ensure the communication process is appropriately applied. As McFarlane emphasizes, "effective communication takes time and requires consideration, thought, and quality time for clear and appropriate construction which incorporates the affective and cognitive elements of spoken language" (p. 2).

What does knowing this information do for the leader? If the leader is aware of what is posited as a fundamental element of effective leadership, they can then be prudent in ensuring that they continually practice the elements of the communication process.

Communication is the most effective weapon that a leader has that can directly impact the organizational objectives. If the leader cannot or chooses not to communicate clearly, the followers are left in a state of chaos, confusion, or isolation. Brown (2009) notes that the best organizations are disciplined, accountable, and strategically aligned with goals due to clear communication from the leaders.

Communication is not something that can be overlooked or avoided if a leader wants to be effective and successful. Communication is a continual learning process with which the leader has to be adaptable and flexible to ensure that they are clear when speaking and that the information is received correctly. This means that the leader not only has to speak, they also have to listen. Listening, just as speaking, involves verbal and non-verbal cues and the leader has to be attuned the characteristics of both. Brown (2009) further suggests, "truly effective communication involves more than just expressing yourself clearly. It also requires effective listening" (p. 8). When a leader executes an effective communication process then the organization and the leader benefits, the leader can expect their followers to execute organizational objectives and goals because the message is clear.

Unfortunately communication skills and the communication process, as discussed in this paper, are not taught within schools. Additionally, Kinnick and Parton (2005) noted many business schools concentrate on an individual's analytical skills instead of honing an individual's communication skill. It is this deficiency that can contribute to an organizational failure or worse a leader's failure. The lessons in business schools and business programs should contain topics on communication processes in its entirety, which includes speaking and listening. These skills should not be taken for granted by leaders or the business schools that educate leaders (Kinnick & Parton, 2005). The global market, that is growing exponentially daily, requires that leaders everywhere be trained with the most current skills to be able to implement organizational strategy, objectives, and mission with minimal effort and have a low tolerance for failure. Failure of these elements due to the leader's inability to communicate effectively could be catastrophic for the leader and the organization.

In today's global marketplace, the competitive landscape ebbs and flows constantly. The swiftest and strong are the ones who capitalize on opportunities while the less fortunate are left to pick over the remains. In stating this, modern technology has changed the way the world communicates by incorporating more electronic means to include social media along with e-mail and other technology. Today's leader has to now exercise their communications and execute the communication process in a variety of ways. Some of the methods that have to be employed leave very little room for interpretation. Due to the varying mechanisms that may be used for communicating, leaders that are not in close proximity to their followers may have a higher level of difficulty achieving communication effectiveness (Neufeld, Zeying, & Yulin, 2010). However, distance between the leader and their followers should not be construed as a pass such that the leader is not still held accountable for effectively communicating. The distance is merely another leadership challenge that must be overcome so that the leader ensures success for themselves and the organization.

The leader must utilize the medium that is available in order to communicate effectively. If social media is all that is available, understand how to use that venue, if electronic mail is one of the methods then ensure that the message is clear before it is sent. "The primary benefit of effective communication and vision setting to leadership is the establishment of a clear purpose leading to efficient and effective decisions and actions" (LaCour & Tissington, 2010, p. 2). The benefits of effective communication to the leader are enormous. As a leader, if they are successful in the communication process then it can be posited that they will be successful in executing the organizational vision and the leader's intentions. The leader has to remember that each listener to the communication is unique and has a listening quality that is individualized to them. It is incumbent upon the leader to understand that and to ensure that the message that is stated is the same message that is received by the listener. LaCour and Tissington (2010) espouses that the leader has to ensure that the message is translated to meet the needs of the listener, which is done through active listening and ensuring that the recipient understands.

Effective communication is not an easy skill to master, it is not substantially taught in schools and it is not normally a focal point for leaders. What is important to glean from this discussion is that effective communication is very important, to the leader and to the organization. To be an effective leader, one that is successful, one has to know that what is spoken is not only heard but also fully understood by the intended audience. LaCour and Tissington (2010) further conclude, "in order to be effective, a leader must communicate to others in a way that the listener's hear" (p. 2.). Succinctly, it is not what the leader says, it is if the leader's message is clearly received and understood that determines organizational outcomes.

References

Baldoni, J. (2004). Powerful leadership communication. *Leader to Leader, 2004*, 20-24.

Brown, W. K. (2009). Listen up. *Professional Safety, 54*, 8-8.

Crainer, S., & Dearlove, D. (2008). The heart of leadership. *Business Strategy Review, 19*, 40-45.

Kinnick, K. N., & Parton, S. R. (2005). Workplace communication. *Business Communication Quarterly, 68*, 429-456.

LaCour, M., & Tissington, L. (2010). What is quality leadership? *Academic Leadership, 8*(3), 1-3.

McFarlane, D. A. (2010). Social communication in a technology-driven society: A philosophical exploration of factor-impacts and consequences. *American Communication Journal, 12*, 1-14.

Neufeld, D. J., Zeying, W., & Yulin, F. (2010). Remote leadership, communication effectiveness and leader performance. *Group Decision & Negotiation, 19*, 227-246. doi:10.1007/s10726-008-9142-x

Appendix A

Suggested Readings

Cline, S. (2005). Soft skills make the difference in the workplace. *Colorado Springs Business Journal.*

Crowe, M. T., & O'Malley, J. (2006). Teaching critical reflection skills for advanced mental health nursing practice: a deconstructive-reconstructive approach. *Journal of Advanced Nursing, 56*(1), 79-87.

Dunphy, H. (2007). Doing business globally. *Network Journal, 14*(6), 28.

Elksnin, L. K., & Elksnin, N. (2003). Fostering social-emotional learning in the classroom. *Education, 124*(1), 63.

Fullam, C., Lando, A., Johansen, M., Reyes, A., & Szaloczy, D. (1998). The triad of empowerment: Leadership, environment, and professional traits. *Nursing Economics, 16*(5), 254-257, 253.

Galagan, P. (2010). Bridging the skills gap: Part II. *Public Manager, 39*(2), 52.

Griggs Jr., F. E. (2009). Everything I needed to know about leadership I learned in the Boy Scouts. *Leadership & Management in Engineering, 9*(4), 198-204. doi: 10.1061/(asce)lm.1943-5630.0000030

Harrigan, K. R., & Dalmia, G. (1991). Knowledge workers: The last bastion of competitive advantage. *Planning Review, 19*(6), 4.

Harris, P. (2007). Holistic skills management comes of age. *T+D, 61*(12), 46.

Jorgensen, H. (2010). Assessing students' technical skill attainment. *Techniques: Connecting Education and Careers, 85*(5), 30-32.

Joshi, R. M., Aaron, P. G., Hill, N., Dean, E. O., Gooden, R. B., & Rupley, W. H. (2008). Drop everything and write (DEAW): An innovative program to improve literacy skills. *Learning Inquiry, 2*(1), 1.

Kar, A. K. (2011). Importance of life skills for the professionals of 21st century. *IUP Journal of Soft Skills, 5*(3), 35-45.

Laszlo, E. (1996). *The systems view of the world: A holistic vision for our time*. Cresskill, NJ: Hampton Press.

Lautenschlager, L., & Smith, C. (2007). Beliefs, knowledge, and values held by inner-city youth about gardening, nutrition, and cooking. *Agriculture and Human Values, 24*, 245-258. doi: 10.1007/s10460-006-9051-z

Levasseur, R. E. (2001). People skills: Change Management tools - Lewin's change model. *Interfaces, 31*(4), 71.

Manee, F. M., Khouiee, S. A., & Zaree, H. (2011). The effect of three life skills instruction on the general health of college freshmen. *Journal of Mazandaran University of Medical Sciences (JMUMS), 21*(85), 127-137.

Philley, J. (2005). Critical thinking concepts. *Professional Safety, 50*(3), 26-32.

Picklesimer, B. K., & Miller, T. K. (1998). Life-skills development inventory-college form: An assessment measure. *Journal of College Student Development, 39*(1), 100-110.

Reilly, R. C. (2006). The use of public reflection to promote workplace learning and expert thinking skills. *International Journal of Learning, 12*(9), 17-31.

Richarme, M. (2009). Ten forces driving business futures. *The Futurist, 43*(4), 40.

Savage, A., & Sales, M. (2008). The anticipatory leader: futurist, strategist and integrator. *Strategy & Leadership, 36*(6), 28.

Sharp, M. (2010). Development of an instrument to measure students' perceptions of information technology fluency skills: Establishing content validity. *Perspectives in Health Information Management, 1.*

Shelton, C. K., & Darling, J. R. (2001). The quantum skills model in management: A new paradigm to enhance effective leadership. *Leadership & Organization Development Journal, 22*(5/6), 264-273.

Shelton, C. D., Hall, R. F., & Darling, J. R. (2003). When cultures collide: The challenge of global integration. *European Business Review, 15*(5), 312.

Stansbury, J., & Victor, B. (2009). Whistle-blowing among young employees: A life-course perspective. *Journal of Business Ethics, 85*(3), 281.

Stokking, K., van der Schaaf, M., Jaspers, J., & Erkens, G. (2004). Teachers' assessment of students' research skills. *British Educational Research Journal, 30*(1), 93-116. doi: 10/1080.01411920310001629983

Thomas, D. C. (2006). Domain and development of cultural intelligence: The importance of mindfulness. *Group & Organization Management, 31*(1), 78. doi: 10.1177/1059601105275266

Thomson, J. (2009). The skills gap and business performance. *Corporate Finance Review, 13*(5), 19.

Tiffan, B. (2009). Are you considered a "high potential?". *Physician Executive, 35*(2), 74.

Trent, R. J. (2004). Team leadership at the 100-foot level. *Team Performance Management, 10*(5/6), 94.

Turnbull, H., Greenwood, R., Tworoger, L., & Golden, C. (2010). Skill deficiencies in diversity and inclusion in organizations: Developing an inclusion skills measurement. *Academy of Strategic Management Journal, 9*(1), 1.

Wardman, K. T. (Ed.). (1994). *Reflections on creating learning organizations*. Cambridge, MA: Pegasus Communications.

Whetten, D. A. (1996). An integrated model for teaching management skills. *Journal of Management Education, 20*(2), 152-181,147.

Yan, M. (2010). How cultural awareness works. *Canadian Issues*, 75.

Yeo, R. (2002). From individual to team learning: Practical perspectives on the learning organisation. *Team Performance Management, 8*(7/8), 157-170.

About the Authors

Matthew Alcindor, D.M.

Dr. Matthew Alcindor is a management consultant, human service professional, trainer, facilitator, and educator with 20 years of diverse experiences in varying human service and non-profit settings in urban areas such as Detroit, Philadelphia, New Newark, Jersey City, New York City, and Washington, DC. He is committed to academic excellence and is an inducted member of the oldest international Honor Society in the social sciences: Pi Gamma Mu. Aside from his work in the Department of Health and Human Services (Social Security Administration), Dr. Alcindor has extensive non-profit experience, having worked in such agencies as Philadelphia's Resources for Human Development (RHD), and New York City's Catholic Guardian Society and Home Bureau (CGSHB). Dr. Alcindor has extensive experience in the child welfare system, having done research in three of the largest child welfare agencies in New York State. His Dissertation, *"Leadership Perceptions in Child Welfare Agencies and their Implications on Retention and Job Satisfaction*," calls attention to subjects such as emotional intelligence.

In the field of service to the developmentally disabled populations, Dr. Alcindor brings extensive experience in management, supervision, clinical coordination, and quality assurance. He is an experienced counselor, intensive case manager, and facilitator of groups and psycho-educational learning sessions. A graduate of Lincoln University's Master of Human Service program, Dr. Alcindor is schooled in the integration of systems theory and thinking with human service and social work practice. He is proficient in processing group and team dynamics. Earning his Doctor of Management in Organizational Leadership from the University of Phoenix School of Advanced Studies, Dr. Alcindor remains committed to lifelong learning and professional development, which he views as the foundation to effective and authentic leadership.

****

Gabriel Flores, Ed.D.

Dr. Gabriel Flores has a Doctor of Education in Educational Leadership and 15 years of classroom experience within the Los Angeles Unified School District (LAUSD). His interests include qualitative research and the inclusion of sexual orientation education within multicultural education programs. He currently works as an adjunct faculty member in the College of Education at University of Phoenix.

****

J. Phillip Harris, D.B.A.

Dr. J. Phillip Harris is the founder and principal of Acclaimed Professionals Group and runs APG Academy of Entrepreneurship, an online consulting and coaching firm. He is an experienced business entrepreneur with a passion for helping others. Dr. Harris has served as chief financial officer in both higher education and manufacturing and has entrepreneurial experience in manufacturing, real estate, and consulting. He is a certified public accountant and practiced as an auditor for a major accounting firm. Dr. Harris teaches and serves as a mentor at the University of Phoenix, specializing in entrepreneurship, finance, and management. He reads and interprets academic journals about business entrepreneurship and finance and engages in writing articles for publication in scholarly journals.

****

Frederick Littles

Frederick Littles was born and raised in Mississippi. As an active duty member of the United States Air Force, he brings extensive practical experience to the Doctor of Management program at the University of Phoenix. After starting his undergraduate work at traditional colleges in Mississippi, he has continued his education at University of Phoenix and not looked back.

****

George W. Rideout, D.B.A.

Dr. George W. Rideout is a principal for Evolution Strategists LLC and executive director of the Change Leadership Intelligence (CLQ) Institute. He holds an MBA and numerous professional certifications, including the certified six-sigma black belt (CSSBB), and the FCIB international certified credit executive

(ICCE). He is a published author and frequent speaker, with more than 16 years' experience in sales and management, leading sales teams in the United States and Canada. His research interests include change leadership, decision-making, leadership studies, multiple intelligences, and systems theories.

****

Edric Spruill, D.M.

Dr. Edric "Rick" Spruill is a proven and tested leadership expert. He received his Doctor of Management degree in Organizational Leadership from the University of Phoenix in 2008. His work includes a case study researching the possible correlation between organizational climate and employee performance and numerous contributions to journals and articles. He is a retired U.S. Army First Sergeant with more than 20 years of active duty and reserve time. During that time he served as Drill Sergeant and Platoon Sergeant, held various titles, and has received numerous awards. Dr. Spruill is a lecturer, a college adjunct faculty member, and coach. He has facilitated teams in team building and communication and coached individuals on career and life goals and decisions. He regularly advises two of his most complex students: his teenage-adult children.

Dr. Spruill espouses the view that situational leadership is the most prominent leadership model in practice today. It is used daily in many organizations throughout the world. Succinctly, he believes and teaches that an effective leader has to ebb and flow between styles in order to continue being productive. In his years serving in many roles in corporations and the Army, he has practiced and preached that concept.

He continues to enjoy discussing and teaching leadership concepts, teaching technology-related courses on the college level, crafting surveys for teams to assess certain quantifiable dynamics, and coaching when called upon. Dr. Spruill has presented for large and small audiences in corporate settings and to all levels within the U.S. Army from generals down to privates. He is adept at engaging the audience as appropriate with the right blend of seriousness and humor to convey the necessary highlights of discussion. He is devoted to his loving wife, three children, and feisty pet dog.

www.ingramcontent.com/pod-product-compliance
Lightning Source LLC
Chambersburg PA
CBHW070531030426
42337CB00016B/2181